CONTENTS

I'd Like to Teach the World to Sing

SECONDO

Words and Music by Bill Backer,
Roquel Davis, Roger Cook
and Roger Greenaway
Arranged by Naoko Ikeda

Moderately, with a slight swing

EASY POP
DUETS 2

8 EXCITING ARRANGEMENTS

BY GLENDA AUSTIN, ERIC BAUMGARTNER,
NAOKO IKEDA, AND CAROLYN MILLER

ISBN 978-1-70515-823-4

WILLIS MUSIC

EXCLUSIVELY DISTRIBUTED BY

HAL•LEONARD®

Visit Hal Leonard Online at
www.halleonard.com

Contact us:
Hal Leonard
7777 West Bluemound Road
Milwaukee, WI 53213
Email: info@halleonard.com

In Europe, contact:
Hal Leonard Europe Limited
42 Wigmore Street
Marylebone, London, W1U 2RN
Email: info@halleonardeurope.com

In Australia, contact:
Hal Leonard Australia Pty. Ltd.
4 Lentara Court
Cheltenham, Victoria, 3192 Australia
Email: info@halleonard.com.au

NOTE TO PERFORMERS

These are pop songs, and many are beloved the world over. But, feel free to give these arrangements your own special seasoning: take liberties with a rhythm or two, sing out loud when you know the lyrics, or repeat the sections you like again and again. Most importantly, have the best time performing with your duet partner!

I'd Like to Teach the World to Sing

PRIMO

Words and Music by Bill Backer,
Roquel Davis, Roger Cook
and Roger Greenaway
Arranged by Naoko Ikeda

Moderately, with a slight swing

SECONDO

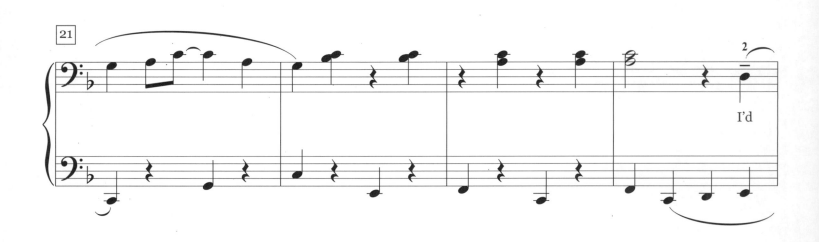

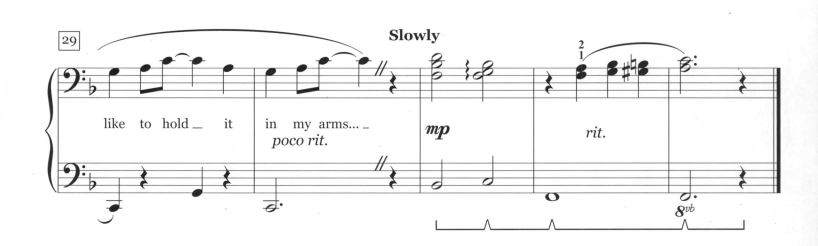

PRIMO

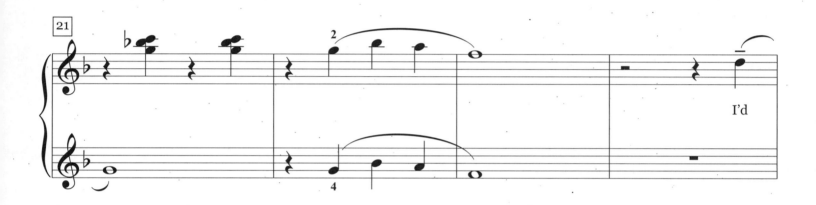

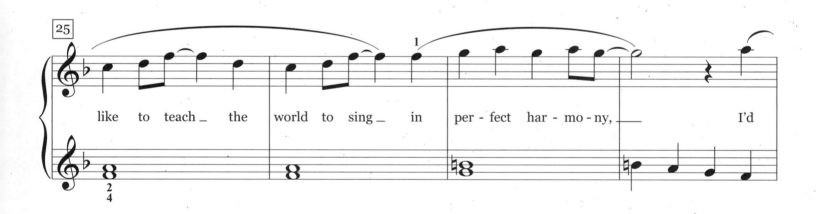

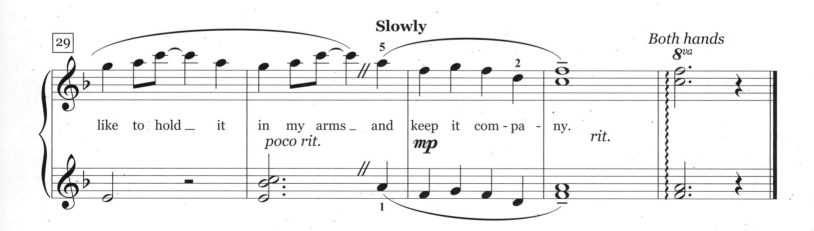

Old Town Road
(I Got the Horses in the Back)

SECONDO

Words and Music by Trent Reznor,
Atticus Ross, Kiowa Roukema
and Montero Lamar Hill
Arranged by Glenda Austin

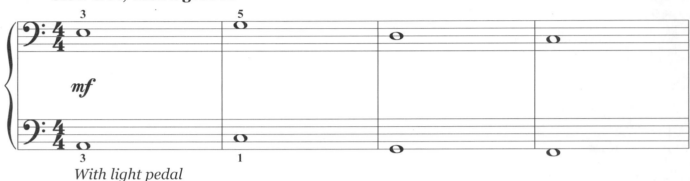

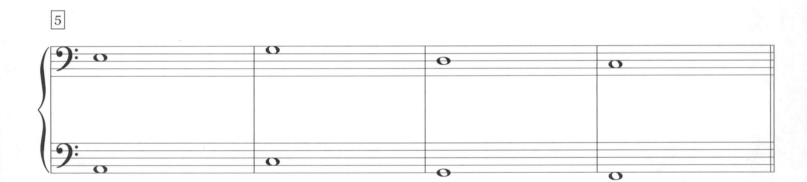

Old Town Road
(I Got the Horses in the Back)

PRIMO

Words and Music by Trent Reznor,
Atticus Ross, Kiowa Roukema
and Montero Lamar Hill
Arranged by Glenda Austin

Slow trot, with a groove

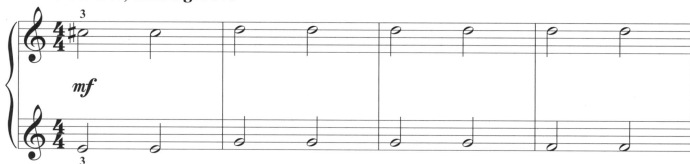

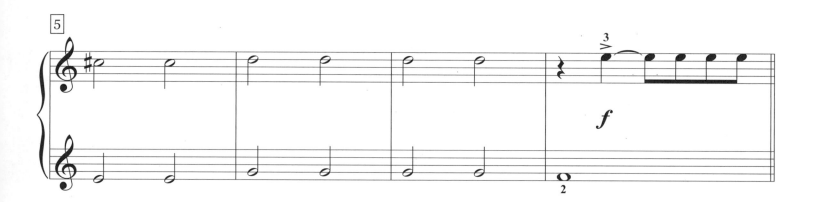

SECONDO

SECONDO

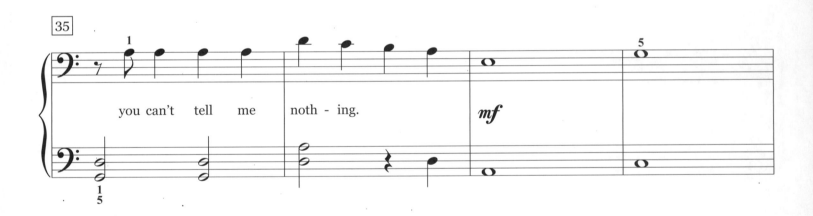

* Chord will clash

PRIMO

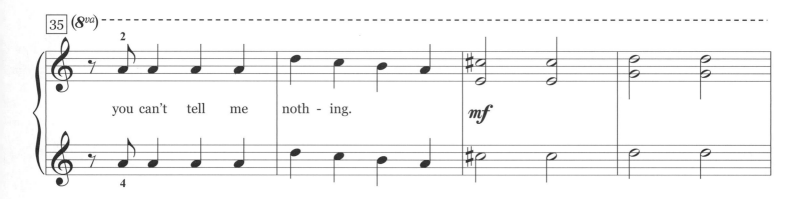

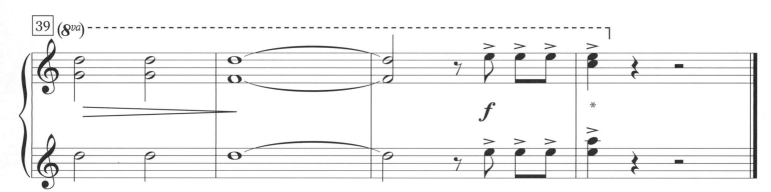

* Chord will clash

We Will Rock You

SECONDO

Words and Music by
Brian May
Arranged by Glenda Austin

With a steady beat

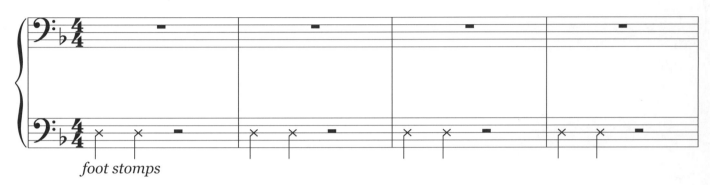

foot stomps

f *strong accents*
throughout

* smaller hands may leave out top note

We Will Rock You

PRIMO

Words and Music by
Brian May
Arranged by Glenda Austin

With a steady beat

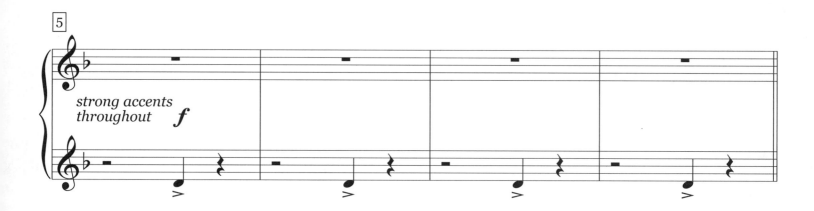

SECONDO

PRIMO

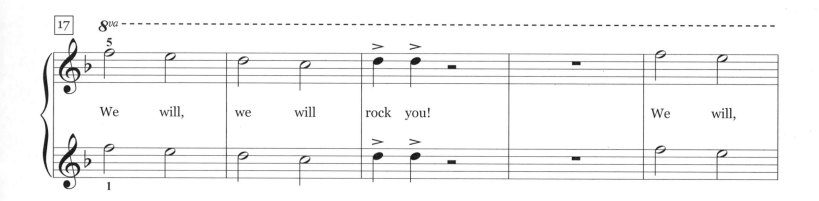

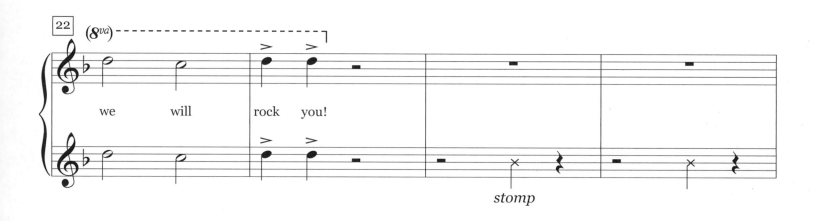

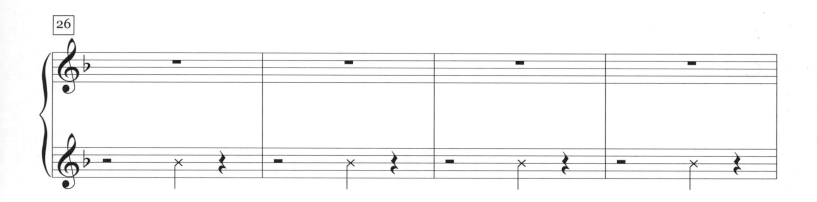

SECONDO

PRIMO

We will,

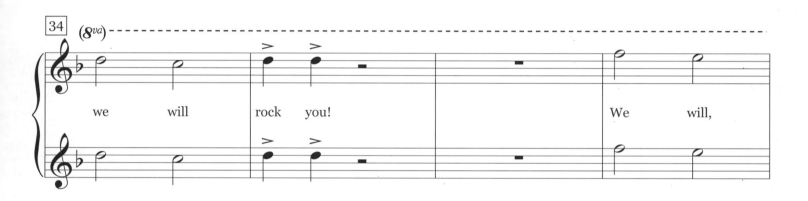

we will   rock   you!   We   will,

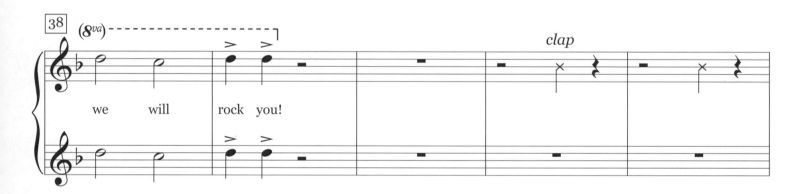

we   will   rock   you!   *clap*

f   *ff*

Butter

SECONDO

**Words and Music by Alexander Joshua Bilowitz,
Namjun Kim, Robert Grimaldi, Jenna Andrews,
Stephen Kirk, Sebastian Garcia and Ron Perry
Arranged by Eric Baumgartner**

Slick Pop feel

Butter

PRIMO

Words and Music by Alexander Joshua Bilowitz,
Namjun Kim, Robert Grimaldi, Jenna Andrews,
Stephen Kirk, Sebastian Garcia and Ron Perry
Arranged by Eric Baumgartner

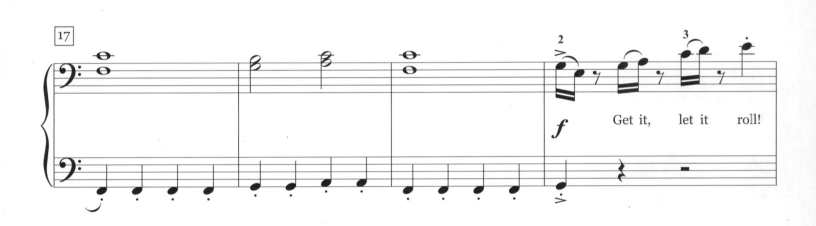

Get it,   let it   roll!

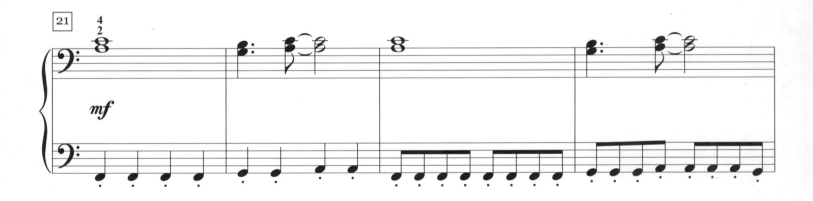

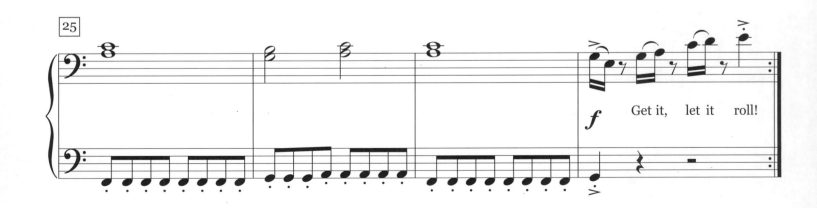

Get it,   let it   roll!

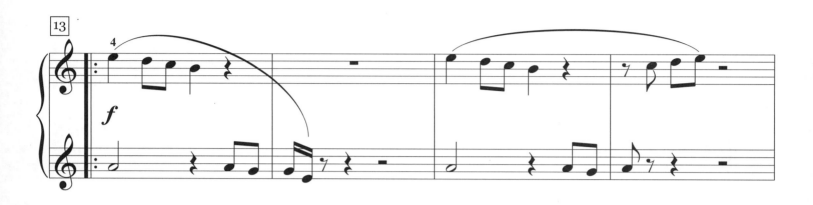

Get it, let it roll!

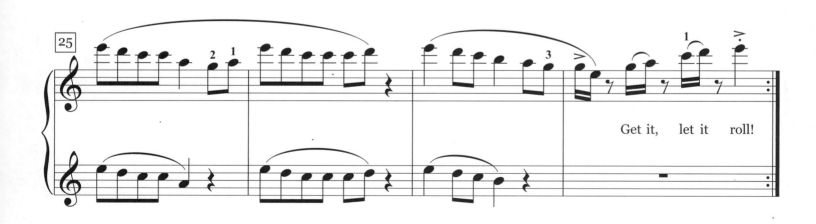

Get it, let it roll!

I Will Always Love You

SECONDO

Words and Music by
Dolly Parton
Arranged by Eric Baumgartner

I Will Always Love You

PRIMO

Words and Music by
Dolly Parton
Arranged by Eric Baumgartner

Tenderly

SECONDO

A-bove all this I wish _ you love. _____

poco rit.

mf a tempo

mp

rit.

Ain't No Mountain High Enough

SECONDO

Words and Music by Nickolas Ashford
and Valerie Simpson
Arranged by Naoko Ikeda

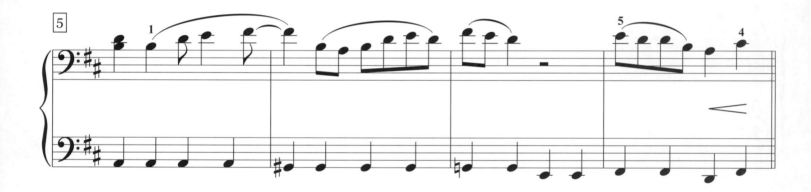

Ain't No Mountain High Enough

PRIMO

Words and Music by Nickolas Ashford
and Valerie Simpson
Arranged by Naoko Ikeda

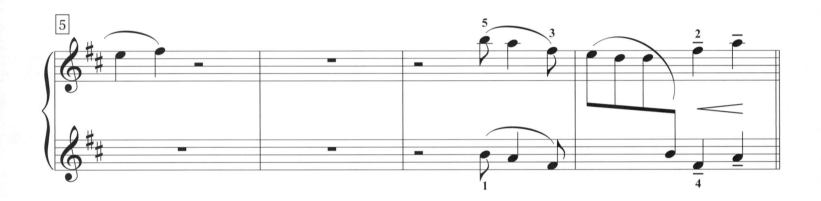

SECONDO

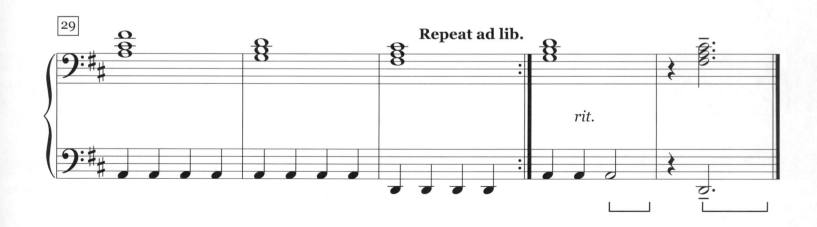

babe.

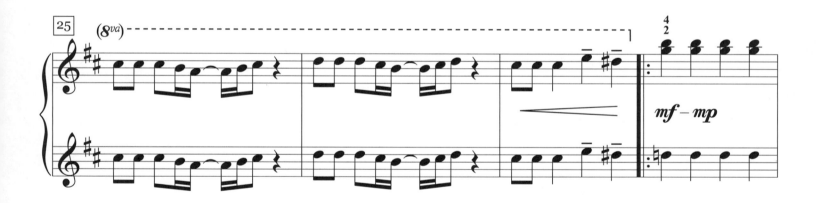

Repeat ad lib.

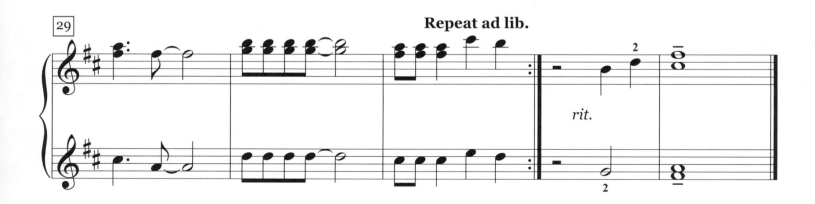

Love Yourself

SECONDO

Words and Music by Justin Bieber,
Benjamin Levin, Ed Sheeran,
Joshua Gudwin and Scott Braun
Arranged by Carolyn Miller

Relaxed Pop groove

Love Yourself

PRIMO

Words and Music by Justin Bieber,
Benjamin Levin, Ed Sheeran,
Joshua Gudwin and Scott Braun
Arranged by Carolyn Miller

Relaxed Pop groove

SECONDO

PRIMO

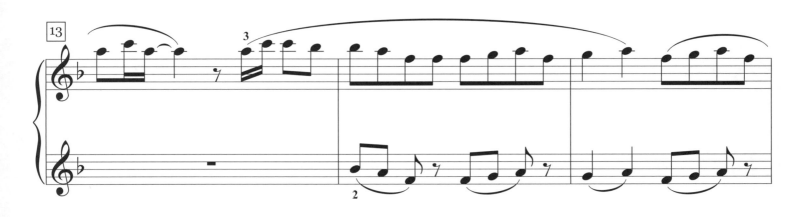

SECONDO

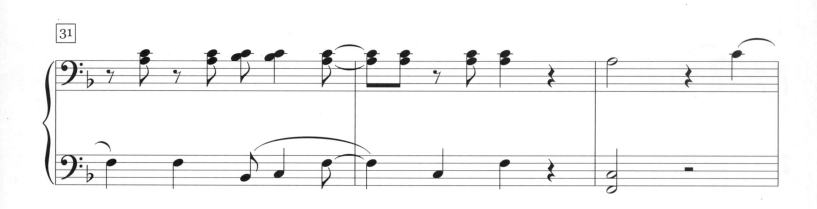

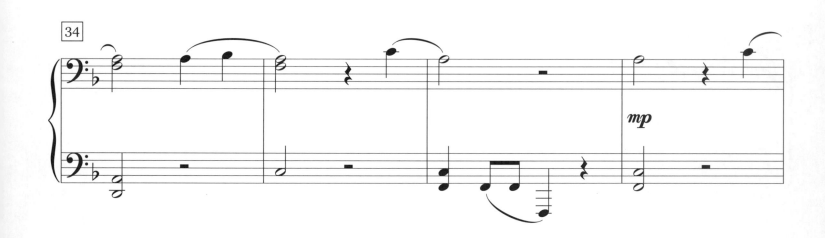

PRIMO

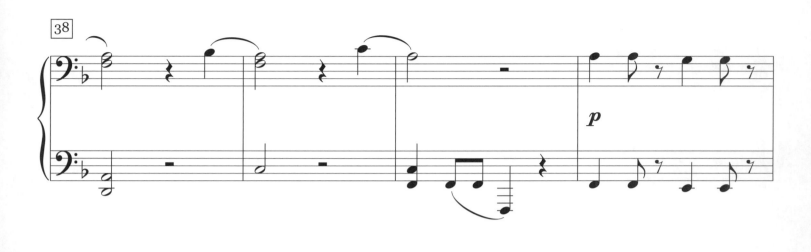

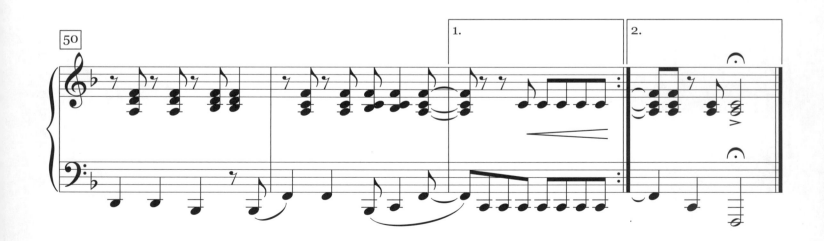

Baby Shark

SECONDO

Traditional Nursery Rhyme
Arranged by Pinkfong and KidzCastle
Arranged by Carolyn Miller

Baby Shark

PRIMO

Traditional Nursery Rhyme
Arranged by Pinkfong and KidzCastle
Arranged by Carolyn Miller

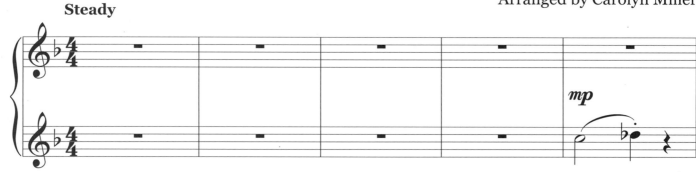

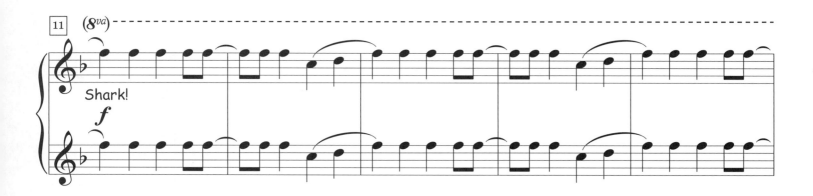

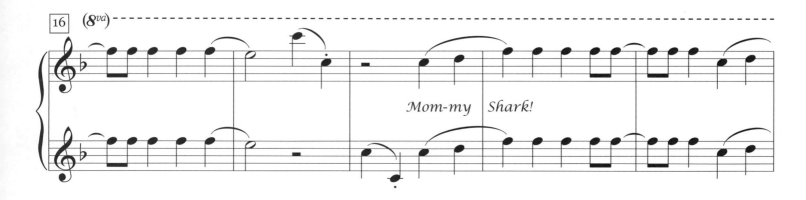

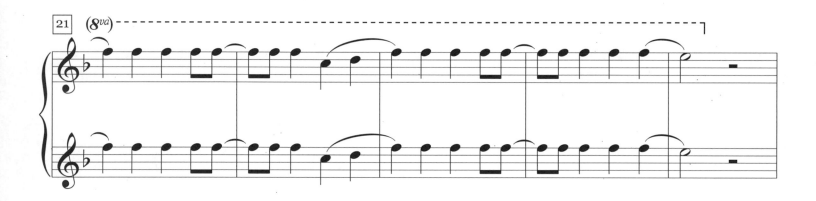

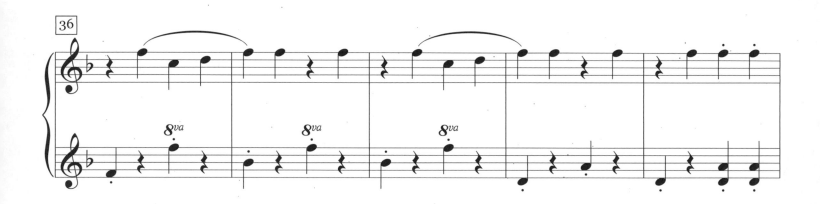

SECONDO

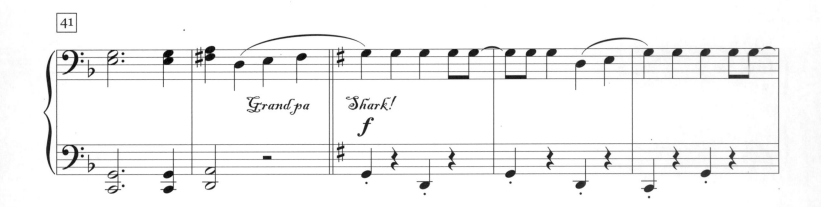

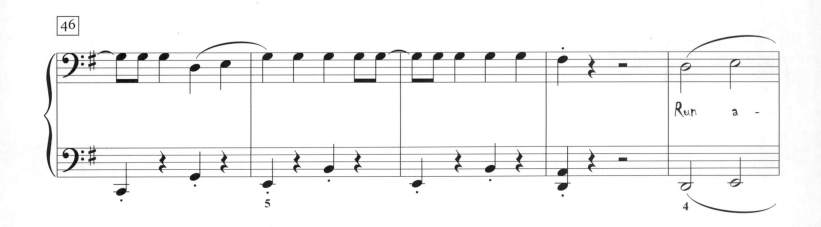

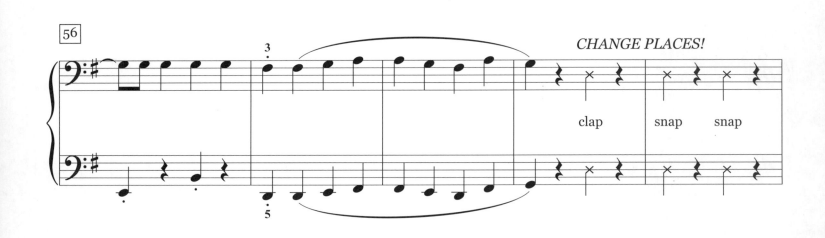

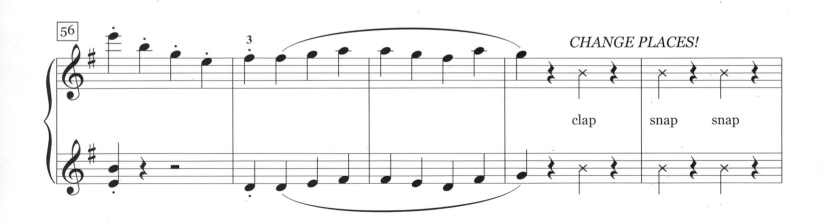

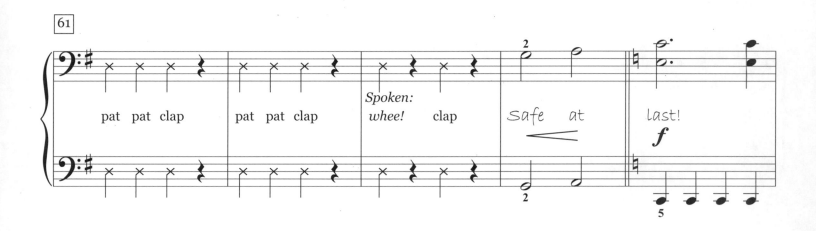

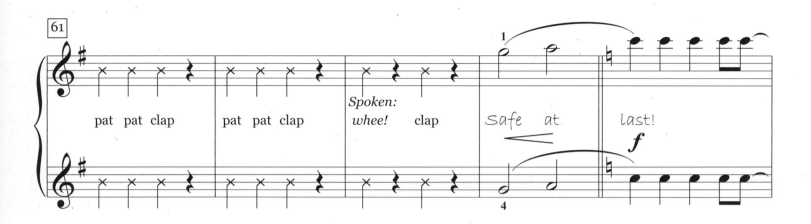

pat pat clap   pat pat clap   *Spoken:* whee!   clap   safe at   last!

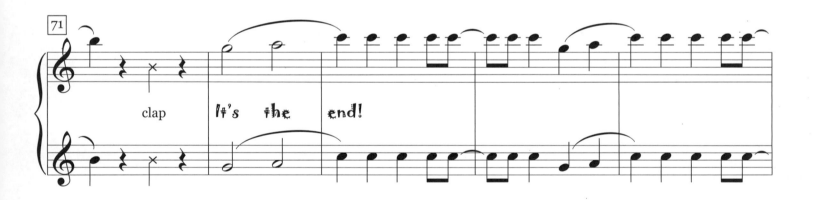

clap   It's the end!

Both hands

Glenda Austin is a pianist, arranger, and composer who writes piano music popular at all levels. She graduated from the University of Missouri (Columbia) with a bachelor's degree in music education and a master's degree in piano performance. Glenda has over 40 years' experience as an elementary and high school music teacher, and holds memberships in the Music Teachers National Association and Missouri Music Educators Association. A frequent adjudicator and clinician, she has presented workshops for teachers and students throughout the United States, as well as in Canada and Japan. In addition, she is collaborative pianist for the choral department at Missouri Southern State University. Married to high-school sweetheart, David, they are the parents of Susan and Scott, and grandparents of Isaac, Eden, and Levi.

Eric Baumgartner received jazz degrees from Berklee College of Music and DePaul University. He is the author and creator of Jazz Piano Basics, a series that presents jazz fundamentals in an accessible manner through short dynamic exercises. Eric is a sought-after clinician who has presented throughout the US, Canada, England, Germany, and Australia. He and his wife Aretta live in Atlanta, Georgia where he maintains an active schedule as performer, composer, and dedicated member of the local music scene.

Naoko Ikeda lives in Sapporo, Hokkaido in northern Japan, and is passionate about introducing the world to her country's essence through music. Influenced by classical music, jazz and pop, as well as the piano works of William Gillock, her own music reflects her diverse tastes with beauty, elegance, and humor. Naoko holds a piano performance degree from Yamaguchi College of Arts in Japan and currently maintains an energetic schedule as both teacher and composer.

Carolyn Miller is a teacher, pianist, and composer from Cincinnati, Ohio. She holds music degrees from the College Conservatory of Music at the University of Cincinnati and Xavier University. She has taught piano to students of all ages for many years, both private and in the classroom, and often adjudicates at music festivals and competitions. Her music teaches essential technical skills, yet is fun to play, which appeals to both children and adults. Many of her compositions appear on contest lists, including the NFMC Festivals Bulletin. Carolyn also directs a large church choir and is the pianist for special services. She enjoys spending time with her husband Gary and their entire family, especially her seven grandchildren.